HIP-HOP

Will Smith

Jim Corrigan

Mason Crest Publishers

Will Smith

Frontis Talented rapper Will Smith has become one of hip-hop's biggest superstars. In addition to his award-winning music, Smith has appeared in highly successful movies and television shows.

Produced by 21st Century Publishing and Communications, Inc.

MASON CREST PUBLISHERS INC.
370 Reed Road
Broomall, Pennsylvania 19008
(866)MCP-BOOK (toll free)
www.masoncrest.com

Printed in Malaysia.

9 8 7 6 5 4 3 2

Library of Congress Cataloging-in-Publication Data

Corrigan, Jim.
    Will Smith / Jim Corrigan.
        p. cm. — (Hip-hop)
    Includes bibliographical references (p.   ), discography (p.   ), filmography (p.   ), and index.
ISBN-13: 978-1-4222-0128-2
ISBN-10: 1-4222-0128-7
    1. Smith, Will, 1968–   —Juvenile literature. 2. Actors—United States—Biography—Juvenile literature. 3. Rap musicians—United States—Biography—Juvenile literature. I. Title. II. Series.
PN2287.S612C67 2007
791.4302'8092—dc22
[B]   2006011442

Publisher's notes:

- All quotations in this book come from original sources, and contain the spelling and grammatical inconsistencies of the original text.

- The Web sites mentioned in this book were active at the time of publication. The publisher is not responsible for Web sites that have changed their addresses or discontinued operation since the date of publication. The publisher will review and update the Web site addresses each time the book is reprinted.

Contents

Hip-Hop Timeline

1974 Hip-hop pioneer Afrika Bambaataa organizes the Universal Zulu Nation.

1988 *Yo! MTV Raps* premieres on MTV.

1970s Hip-hop as a cultural movement begins in the Bronx, New York City.

1985 *Krush Groove*, a hip-hop film about Def Jam Recordings, is released featuring Run-D.M.C., Kurtis Blow, LL Cool J, and the Beastie Boys.

1970s DJ Kool Herc pioneers the use of breaks, isolations, and repeats using two turntables.

1979 The Sugarhill Gang's song "Rapper's Delight" is the first hip-hop single to go gold.

1986 Run-D.M.C. are the first rappers to appear on the cover of *Rolling Stone* magazine.

1970   1980   1988

1976 Grandmaster Flash & the Furious Five pioneer hip-hop MCing and freestyle battles.

1986 Beastie Boys' album *Licensed to Ill* is released and becomes the best-selling rap album of the 1980s.

1970s Break dancing emerges at parties and in public places in New York City.

1982 Afrika Bambaataa embarks on the first European hip-hop tour.

1988 Hip-hop music annual record sales reaches $100 million.

1970s Graffiti artist Vic pioneers tagging on subway trains in New York City.

1984 *Graffiti Rock*, the first hip-hop television program, premieres.

1993 Rapper Snoop Dogg's album *Doggystyle* is the first debut album to hit the music charts at number one.

2006 Queen Latifah becomes the first hip-hop artist to receive a star on the Hollywood Walk of Fame.

1989 DJ Jazzy Jeff & The Fresh Prince become the first hip-hop artists to win a Grammy Award.

2003 Rapper Eminem becomes the first hip-hop artist to win an Academy Award.

2005 Hip-hop artist Kanye West appears on the cover of *Time* magazine.

1989 Rap is added as a new category to the *Billboard* charts.

1997 East Coast rapper Notorious B.I.G. (aka Biggie Smalls) is murdered.

2004 First National Hip-Hop Political Convention is held in Newark, New Jersey.

1989   2000   2006

1990s Hip-hop emerges in Europe.

1996 West Coast rapper Tupac Shakur is shot and killed.

2005 Rapper Will Smith opens the Philadelphia Live 8 concert as part of 10 simultaneous concerts held worldwide to bring attention to the extreme poverty in Africa.

1989 First gangsta rap album, *Straight Outta Compton*, is released by N.W.A.

2001 The hip-hop political action group, Hip-Hop Summit Action Network, is founded by Russell Simmons.

1992 Dr. Dre's album *The Chronic* is released; it redefines West Coast rap.

2006 The Smithsonian Institute National Museum of American History announces the creation of a new hip-hop exhibition scheduled to open in three to five years.

Because of his status as one of America's most recognizable music stars, Will Smith was chosen to open the Live 8 concert in Philadelphia. The enormous crowd cheered as he took the stage on July 2, 2005, at the Philadelphia Museum of Art.

Meet Will Smith

Nearly a million people cheered loudly as Will Smith appeared on stage. It was July 2, 2005, and Will was hosting the Live 8 concert in his hometown of Philadelphia. All around the world, millions of people were watching the concert via satellite. It was the latest evidence that Will Smith was an international superstar.

Yet Will was not hosting the concert to enhance his own fame. He was doing it for charity. The Live 8 concert series was designed to raise public awareness of poverty in Africa. Other Live 8 concerts were being held at the same time in cities all across the globe. "Right now you're watching the biggest concert event in the history of the world," Will told his international audience.

Live 8 concerts were taking place in London, Moscow, Rome, Paris, and elsewhere. A total of more than 1,000 musicians would perform at the 11 concerts. Over 2,000 television and radio networks would broadcast the event. Concert organizers were hoping to persuade eight of the world's most powerful nations to give Africa more aid. Those nations, commonly known as the G8, are Canada, France, Germany, Italy, Japan, Russia, the United Kingdom, and the United States.

Will Smith was already well aware of the widespread suffering in Africa. He learned much about the continent's plight while filming a movie there in 2001. Since that time, Will has worked to ease poverty and stop the spread of AIDS in Africa.

Finger Snap

At Live 8, Will had a special way of teaching his global audience about Africa's anguish. He explained that once every three seconds an African child dies from poverty. To demonstrate just how often that was, Will asked everyone in the crowd to snap their fingers once every three seconds. He solemnly led the way as people from across North America and Europe snapped their fingers in unison, each snap marking a death. It was a powerful and sobering lesson.

Several days after the concerts, leaders from the G8 nations pledged to increase their aid to Africa. There is no way of knowing exactly how much the Live 8 concerts influenced their decision. Many other groups and individuals had also worked to increase awareness of African poverty. However, there could be little doubt that the Live 8 organizers and performers had achieved their goal.

Live 8 was special because it accomplished its charitable mission through music. In London, performers such as Snoop Dogg, Madonna, and Mariah Carey entertained the audience. Bands like Audioslave and Green Day rocked the stage in Berlin. Country stars Tim McGraw and Faith Hill were part of the lineup in Rome. There was something for music lovers of every kind.

Philadelphia's Live 8 concert was particularly special for fans of hip-hop. As the host, Will Smith gave the concert a unique hip-hop flavor. Additionally, there were performances by Kanye West, Jay-Z, and the Black-Eyed Peas. At one point, Will took a break from his **emcee** duties to perform on stage. With his longtime musical partner, DJ Jazzy Jeff, Will thrilled the crowd with such hits as "Gettin' Jiggy Wit It" and "Summertime." The show ended with a performance by rhythm and blues legend Stevie Wonder.

More than a million people watched Will Smith's performance at the Live 8 concert in Philadelphia. The purpose of the show, part of a series of concerts staged all around the world, was to pressure the industrialized world to end African poverty.

An Early Start

Will Smith was 36 years old when he hosted the Live 8 concert. At that age, he had already achieved more success than he could have possibly imagined. But all of the money and fame has not gone to his head. Many people who know Will say he still has the same friendly and easygoing attitude today that he had as a boy.

Will's rise to stardom began almost two decades earlier on the streets of West Philadelphia, not far from where the Live 8 concert was held. He knew from an early age that he loved music and that he loved to perform for people. At that time, in the mid-1980s, rap or hip-hop music was just gaining popularity with Philadelphia's youth. Will was no exception, and soon he was not only listening to hip-hop music, but also composing raps of his own.

DJ Jazzy Jeff (back) works the turntables while Will Smith raps at a show in New York's Rockefeller Center. The partners, who had a string of hits in the 1980s and early 1990s, reunited for several songs on Smith's 2005 album *Lost & Found*.

Will began performing at street parties, and he soon had a reputation as a talented rapper. But it was not until he teamed up with Jeff Townes that his musical career really took off. As DJ Jazzy Jeff & The Fresh Prince, the two friends began creating music that was unique and special.

Some rap lyrics had a serious or negative theme, but Will's songs were always funny and upbeat. He sang about amusing episodes in his life, such as shopping for clothes with his parents. His raps told interesting stories that young people could relate to, regardless of their background. DJ Jazzy Jeff & The Fresh Prince would go on to have many hits, and even win the first Grammy ever awarded for rap music. Will's talent and charisma eventually led him into a major acting career in television and film.

Today, Will Smith continues to make music and movies. He is also a husband, a father, and a **philanthropist**. The story of how Will evolved from street-corner rapper into global celebrity is a fascinating one. Along the way, he achieved many great triumphs, but also made several mistakes, which he has made sure never to repeat. Will credits his parents with teaching him to work hard and to never stop trying.

Will Smith accompanies his mother, Caroline, to an awards ceremony in France, 2005. Although the Smith family was by no means wealthy, both Caroline and Willard Smith Sr. worked hard and did their best to provide a good home for their children.

2

The Fresh Prince Is Born

I n high school, Will Smith was the class clown. "I'd cut up the class but still take in what the teacher was saying," he told *People* magazine in 1996. Despite his antics, Will's easy smile and smooth talk usually kept him out of trouble. As a result, some teachers began calling him Prince Charming.

Will's classmates eventually shortened his nickname to Prince. When he began rapping, it became part of his stage name: Fresh Prince. "Fresh" was a popular substitute for "cool." But no matter how cool the young rapper may have thought he was, he would always be just plain Will to his family.

The Smith family lived in West Philadelphia, in a pleasant neighborhood known as Wynnefield. Will grew up with an older sister, Pam, and two younger siblings, twins Ellen and Harry. His father, Willard C. Smith Sr., ran a business that provided refrigeration to supermarkets. Will's mother, Caroline, was a school board administrator.

From the time he was very young, Will showed an **aptitude** for words. His mother claimed that he could talk before he could walk. He enjoyed books, especially the quirky, rhyming stories of Dr. Seuss. In grade school, he dabbled at writing poetry. "Words and rhymes got me going," he explained to *Essence*. "So as a young teenager, I fell into rap. It was a natural progression."

When Will was 10 years old, he received his first stereo system. While listening to its radio one evening, he heard a tune called "Rapper's Delight" by the Sugar Hill Gang. Although he may not have realized it at the time, he was listening to the very first hip-hop hit. "Rapper's Delight" was witty, unique, and funny, and Will was captivated by it. He immediately began putting together his own raps.

Will's early attempts imitated the tough, streetwise rap lyrics of the time. Some rappers used profanity in their songs, so he did the same. That all changed after his grandmother found the notebook containing his lyrics. She told him he was too intelligent to use such language. Will took the lesson to heart and vowed that he would never again write anything that might embarrass his family.

Building a Reputation

Will started performing on street corners and at neighborhood house parties. Rappers often competed to see who had the best rhymes, and Will won more than his share of contests. By age 13, he was being paid to perform. He teamed up with a friend, Clarence Holmes, who went by the name Ready Rock-C. Holmes was a human beat box. He could create beats, rhythms, and melodies with his mouth, imitating the sounds of drums, horns, strings, and sound effects. Human beat boxes were an important part of most hip-hop acts in the early and mid-1980s.

As time passed and the duo improved, Will approached a local record producer with a few of their songs. The producer declined the offer, but told Will and Ready Rock-C that they had talent. Despite being turned down, Will was elated by the producer's compliment. He immediately went to work writing more lyrics.

By 1986, Will was entering his senior year at Overbrook High School. Hip-hop had become a major part of his life, and it was much

MUSIC ALIVE!

Bringing Today's Music to the Classroom

Hail to Hip-Hop!

PLUS
JESSICA SIMPSON
COPYRIGHTS
MUSIC IN PERU

BIRTH OF OLD SCHOOL

OCTOBER 2004   Vol. 24 • No. 1

This magazine cover pictures members of the Sugar Hill Gang, a group that influenced many young rappers like Will Smith. Their 1979 song "Rapper's Delight" was the first hip-hop single to hit *Billboard* magazine's Top 40 chart.

more important to him than his schoolwork. But his mother and father insisted that he keep up his grades because they wanted him to go to college. When he wasn't studying, Will devoted his time to music.

A few years earlier, Will's parents had separated. But although Will's father no longer lived in the Smith household, he continued to play an important role in his children's lives. "What my father always made very clear to me is just do one thing well, just make sure you can focus," Will recalled in an interview with *Jet*. "If you do one thing well, everything else will come from that."

To prove his point, Will's father took his son to work with him in the summertime. Installing refrigeration cases in supermarkets was hard and dirty work. Will marveled at the energy and determination that his father put into the job.

But Willard Smith Sr. was not finished demonstrating the value of hard work. One summer, he told Will and younger brother Harry to replace a crumbling brick wall on the family property. Mixing cement and laying bricks was exhausting labor, and they progressed very slowly, laying one brick at a time. But their father would not let them quit. When summer turned into fall, they continued to work on the project after school.

When it was finally finished and the two boys stood back admiring their handiwork, their father told them that it proved they could do anything if they tried hard enough. Will never forgot the lesson. He told *Ebony* magazine, "I look back on that a lot of times in my life when I think I won't be able to do something, and I tell myself, 'One brick at a time.'"

The Perfect Partnership

Will was not the only hip-hop performer in Philadelphia building a powerful reputation. Jeff Townes had been scratching out sounds as a DJ since he was 10 years old. Unlike most other DJs, Jeff was a huge fan of jazz music, and he often sampled it on his turntables, producing a unique sound. His stage name, DJ Jazzy Jeff, described him perfectly. Jeff's special talents even earned him an appearance on a local radio show.

In 1986, Jeff played at a house party in Will's neighborhood. Almost **spontaneously**, they joined forces on stage and began playing off one another. Rapper and DJ were both thrilled. It was as if Will's words and Jeff's music were made to go together. They immediately became partners and started mixing new songs in Jeff's basement.

Willard Smith Sr. accompanies his famous son and his grand-children to an event in Los Angeles, 2003. Willard was an important role model for Will and his brothers and sisters. He taught that success comes through hard work.

DJ Jazzy Jeff & The Fresh Prince had no trouble getting a record deal, and they quickly released their first single. In "Girls Ain't Nothing But Trouble," Will delivered a humorous rap about disastrous dates, while Jeff sampled the theme song from the television show "I Dream of Jeannie." The song was an instant hit, selling more than 100,000 copies. Teens in America and the United Kingdom enjoyed the song's funny lyrics and quirky melody. But Will and Jeff were just getting

Will met Jeff Townes, who was known as DJ Jazzy Jeff, at a party in 1986, and the two musicians immediately clicked. They enjoyed getting together at Jeff's house after school and creating music together.

started. As "Girls Ain't Nothing But Trouble" climbed the charts, they finished recording their first album.

Their **debut** album, *Rock the House*, arrived in music stores in early 1987. It contained the single "Parents Just Don't Understand," a song that would propel DJ Jazzy Jeff & The Fresh Prince to stardom. Just like their previous hit, "Parents Just Don't Understand" was clever and catchy. Will's lyrics touched on a subject familiar to all teens—coping with stubborn parents. His rhymes told comical stories, such as a disastrous shopping trip with his mother to buy school clothes.

Will and Jeff shot a video for "Parents Just Don't Understand," which MTV played repeatedly. The national television exposure boosted album sales even further. Over half a million copies of *Rock the House* were sold, making it what the music industry calls a gold album.

In addition to sales, DJ Jazzy Jeff & The Fresh Prince were also receiving awards for their music. They won American Music Awards for Best Rap Album and Best Rap Artist. At the 1989 Grammy Awards, "Parents Just Don't Understand" was named Best Rap Performance. It was the first time a Grammy had ever been awarded for rap music.

DJ Jazzy Jeff & The Fresh Prince were awash in money and **accolades**. Will spent lavishly, ignoring his parents' advice to save. Within two years, he would be flat broke and living back at home.

Will Smith, in his colorful Fresh Prince persona, poses with a boom box, circa 1988. Smith and DJ Jazzy Jeff became millionaires thanks to hits like "Girls Ain't Nothing But Trouble," "Parents Just Don't Understand," and "Summertime."

3

Will Goes to Hollywood

At 20 years old, Will Smith was on top of the world. DJ Jazzy Jeff & The Fresh Prince had built an army of loyal fans. Previously, hip-hop was popular only in large cities. But the lighthearted music of Will and Jeff appealed to young people everywhere. The two young men had become millionaires.

Their follow-up album, *He's the DJ, I'm the Rapper*, sold more than 2.5 million copies. Will and Jeff went on an international tour, stopping in London, Moscow, and Japan. They also set up a telephone line where, for a fee, fans could listen to recorded messages from the duo. The line received over two million phone calls in its first six months alone. There was no World Wide Web in 1990, so the call-in line was the most direct way for the artists to send messages to their fans.

Will's bank account swelled with income from album sales, concert receipts, and telephone fees. By age 20, he had earned over a million dollars. But he was spending the money almost as fast as it came in. Will purchased a mansion in the Philadelphia suburbs and filled its garage with six cars. He constantly took his friends out to dinner at the most expensive restaurants he could find. He spent enormous sums of money on custom jewelry and clothing. Once, he and his friends got a Gucci store to lock its doors so they could have a private shopping spree. "Money disappears a lot faster than it comes in, no matter how much you make. Being able to buy anything you want makes you a little crazy," Will later admitted to *People.*

Eventually, the river of cash streaming into Will's bank account began to run dry. DJ Jazzy Jeff & The Fresh Prince's third album, titled *And in This Corner . . .* , achieved gold status, but was not nearly as successful as their second album had been. As the 1990s began, it appeared that fans of DJ Jazzy Jeff & The Fresh Prince were beginning to lose interest.

Even worse, during this time Will learned he had a tax problem. Because he never hired an accountant to handle his money, nobody had been paying the necessary taxes to the government. Will foolishly assumed that the companies sending him checks were handling those details. He was shocked to discover that he owed the government more than a million dollars in overdue taxes.

To help pay off the enormous debt, Will sold his cars and his mansion and moved back into his mother's house. It was a difficult time for the Fresh Prince. He had ignored his parents' warnings about wasting money, and now it appeared they had been right. For the first time since his hip-hop career started, it seemed like their advice about getting a college degree might have been equally as correct. After graduating high school Will had been recruited by the prestigious Massachusetts Institute of Technology, but he turned it down to pursue music—a career that now seemed to be going nowhere.

A Fresh Start

The one thing Will still had working in his favor was his fame. Millions of young people had seen his face repeatedly on MTV. And unlike some other hip-hop artists of the time, Will was regarded as friendly and sincere. He decided to go to Hollywood and see if he could draw on his good reputation to start an acting career.

Luckily for Will, the perfect role was waiting for him. Shortly after arriving in Los Angeles, Will met with a record company executive named Benny Medina. Although Medina worked in the music industry, he was looking to create a television show based on his life as a teenager.

Medina had known poverty as a child, living with his single mother in a troubled Los Angeles neighborhood. When his mother died, he was constantly moving between various foster homes. But Medina's life changed dramatically at age 15, when he moved in with a kind—and wealthy—Beverly Hills family. Although grateful, the tough street kid

This photo of the cast of *The Fresh Prince of Bel-Air* includes star Will Smith in the center. The television series was very successful. Nearly 150 episodes were produced, and it aired on NBC from 1990 to 1996.

suddenly felt strangely out of place in his new environment. As an adult, Medina felt the story about adjusting to the new lifestyle would make a hilarious TV show. Medina convinced a respected music producer and **impresario** named Quincy Jones to help develop the show.

Both Medina and Jones were impressed with Will's audition. Medina thought Will would be perfect for the starring role, and television executives at NBC agreed. The series was dubbed *The Fresh Prince of Bel-Air*, and Will would play a character named after himself. Essentially, Will's character was a wisecracking teen who got into trouble on the streets of Philadelphia. To set him straight, his mother sent him off to live with his rich California relatives. The cultural differences between Will and his hosts, the Banks family, were the show's main source of humor.

The Fresh Prince of Bel-Air offered Will a new chance at success. But he was terrified. He had no acting experience, aside from the clowning around he and Jeff had done in their music videos. He studied his lines and hoped for the best. Afraid of missing his cues, he often mouthed the other actors' lines.

Although Will lacked experience, he made up for it with his enthusiasm and natural charm. While taping the show's first few episodes, he watched his more experienced costars and asked them for acting tips. *The Fresh Prince of Bel-Air* debuted in September 1990, just weeks before Will's 22nd birthday. The show's ratings convinced NBC that it would be a hit, and more episodes were ordered. Will Smith's gamble had paid off, and he had successfully launched his acting career.

Lessons Learned

Will was determined to learn from the mistakes of his past. This time he would not spend his earnings **frivolously**. He moved into a modest Los Angeles apartment and lived sensibly, avoiding expensive restaurants and stores. He committed himself to his work. During the day, Smith spent his time shooting *The Fresh Prince of Bel-Air*. At night, he worked with Jeff on their fourth album, *Homebase*. "I work hard. I work very hard. A lot of times people say some people are just lucky. I don't consider my success luck," Smith told *Ebony*.

The 1991 release of *Homebase* revealed a different side of DJ Jazzy Jeff & The Fresh Prince. The duo had matured somewhat. Their songs were still playful and fun, but with a more sophisticated tone. In the album's biggest hit, a relaxed tune called "Summertime," Will calmly reminisced about the summers of his youth:

> **"school is out and it's a sort of a buzz**
> **a back then I didn't really know what it was**
> **but now I see what have of this**
> **the way that people respond to summer madness**
> **the weather is hot and girls are dressing less**
> **and checking out the fellas to tell 'em who's best**
> **riding around in your jeep or your benzos**
> **or in your nissan sitting on lorenzos**
> **back in philly we be out in the park**
> **a place called the plateau is where everybody goes"**

Listeners of all ages adored the song's smooth melody. "Summertime" was DJ Jazzy Jeff & The Fresh Prince's first and only Top Five pop hit in the United States. It also garnered them their second Grammy Award. This success demonstrated that Will Smith was still a hip-hop star, in addition to being an actor.

As Will's television show continued to gain in popularity, he began receiving offers to make movies. Movies were far more challenging to make than a television show, however, so Will decided to start out slowly. He wanted the chance to hone his acting skills.

Smith began his film career with a small role in the 1992 drama *Where the Day Takes You.* It was a grim story about homeless teenagers, and Will played a young man who could not walk. The following year he took another minor role, this time in the comedy *Made in America.* Although the parts were small, Will was learning and having fun. "I enjoy making movies," he told *Ebony* magazine in 1996. "It allows you to be someone different every time you step up to the camera. You know, television is a **medium** designed for mediocrity, whereas when you're making a film, you have more of an opportunity to achieve aesthetic perfection."

The year 1993 proved to be a turning point in Will's professional career. It was then that he landed his first starring role on the big screen. In the film *Six Degrees of Separation,* which was based on a true story, Will played a gay con artist who called himself Paul Poitier, pretending to be the son of groundbreaking actor Sidney Poitier. The movie was adapted from a play, which was evident in the dense,

Will Smith, accompanied by members of his family, attends the premiere of *Made in America*, May 1993. Will had a very small part in the movie, which starred Ted Danson, Whoopi Goldberg, and Nia Long.

sometimes unnatural dialogue. Will costarred with Golden Globe winner Donald Sutherland and Academy Award nominee Stockard Channing. *Six Degrees* was generally well liked, and Will's performance received encouraging reviews. During that same year, he became executive producer of *The Fresh Prince of Bel-Air*, which gave him more creative control over the show.

It was also in 1993 that DJ Jazzy Jeff & The Fresh Prince released their fifth and final album together, *Code Red*. The release was a major disappointment. The song "Boom! Shake the Room" was a minor hit in the United States and a number one single in the United Kingdom. But otherwise the album was a dismal failure.

Smith decided to focus on his acting instead of his music. He felt that the entire hip-hop **genre** had become something different. Rather than being fun and uplifting, hip-hop in the mid-1990s seemed angry

As a con man who calls himself Paul Poitier, Smith charmed a wealthy white couple played by Stockard Channing (left) and Donald Sutherland (right) in the movie *Six Degrees of Separation*. Overall, movie critics praised Smith's performance.

and violent. Gangsta rap, which venerated violence, drugs, and death, had become the predominant style. In 1993, Smith told *Essence*, "[Hip-hop] has taken a negative turn—glorifying ignorance, violence and misogyny. It's about hate, and that's one thing I don't understand." He later echoed this sentiment in an interview with *Ebony*. "It's gone beyond reality, and it's some kind of bizarre, sick reality that just, I just don't know, it's no good at all," he said. "I think I'm kind of retired from music."

Will and Sheree Smith pose with their son, Trey. In "Just the Two of Us," Will expressed his feelings about fatherhood: "From the first time the doctor placed you in my arms, I knew I'd meet death before I'd let you meet harm."

4

A Period of Changes

During the early 1990s, Will Smith's personal life was just as satisfying as his acting career. In 1992 he married his girlfriend, Sheree Zampino, and in November of that year they had a baby boy. They named their son Willard C. Smith III, but usually called him by his nickname Trey, meaning "three."

The overwhelming joy and responsibility of fatherhood were a shock to Will. "When the doctor handed him to me, I realized things were different now," he said in an interview with *People*. Will later commemorated those initial moments with his son in a rap called "Just the Two of Us." From the time he was just a few months old, Trey was a regular visitor to the set of *The Fresh Prince of Bel-Air*.

As the show's star and executive producer, Smith worked long hours, both in front of and behind the camera. He wanted to take the show in a new direction. Specifically, he wanted to move beyond simple comedy and address some serious social issues, such as drug abuse and teen pregnancy. The executives at NBC, however, were reluctant to change anything on their hit show. Will was able to add a few serious moments to certain episodes, but overall the show remained a comedy.

Smith also used the show to maintain old friendships and develop new ones. For example, he included former musical partner Jeff Townes as a cast member. Jeff appeared in a number of episodes as the mischievous character named Jazz. Also through the show, Will met actress Jada Pinkett. She auditioned to play Will's girlfriend but was passed over for the part because of her height. At just five feet tall, Pinkett looked out of place on the television screen next to Smith's six-foot-two-inch frame. But the two became good friends and stayed in touch.

A Movie Star

Will Smith already knew what it felt like to be a top musical performer. He also knew what it meant to be a network television star. After a few small roles in minor films, by 1995 Will felt confident enough in his acting abilities to star in a major film.

Will's first lead role was in a 1995 action-comedy called *Bad Boys*. Will and his costar, comedian Martin Lawrence, played Miami police detectives working frantically to solve a case and protect a murder witness. Critics did not think the movie was very good, but they were impressed with Will's acting. *Bad Boys* was a box office hit, with worldwide ticket sales of more than $140 million.

A year later, Will starred in the big-budget film *Independence Day*. His character was a high-flying Marine fighter pilot who helped fight off an alien invasion. The movie was the biggest hit of the year, earning more than $300 million just in the United States. Again, Will received critical acclaim for his charismatic performance.

Farewell to the Fresh Prince

By the mid-1990s, it was clear to Will that his television show was winding down. Ideas for new storylines were becoming scarce, and he was forced to admit that he had grown bored with the series. "You're pretty much one character, and there are not many peaks and valleys, just pretty much the same old same old," Will explained to *Ebony* magazine. "I wanted to go out solid, while we were still funny."

In *Bad Boys* (1995), Will Smith starred with comedian Martin Lawrence as police officers trying to protect a witness played by Téa Leoni. The action movie was a summer success, and led to more starring roles for Smith.

For Will, the end of the show also meant the end of his Fresh Prince **persona**. He no longer identified with the high-spirited rapper of his youth. "All the things the Fresh Prince stood for, all the fun he had, still exist inside me," he told *People*. "Those just aren't the dominant aspects of my personality anymore. The Fresh Prince can still come over for dinner, but he has to go home after he eats."

The new sense of maturity that Smith was feeling had no doubt been shaped by events in his private life. In 1995, just as his film career was taking off, he and wife Sheree separated. Shortly afterward they filed for divorce. Will refused to publicly discuss the reasons for their breakup, only hinting that perhaps they had married before they were ready. Regardless, Will vowed to remain a guiding force in the life of his son, Trey, just as his own father had done after he and Will's mother had divorced.

In May 1996, after six successful seasons on the air, *The Fresh Prince of Bel-Air* came to an end. In the final episode, the Banks family sold their mansion and each character bid the others farewell and prepared to begin an exciting new phase in their lives. More than a decade later, *The Fresh Prince of Bel-Air* continues to have a loyal following and the show is broadcast regularly on cable television.

Big Willie Weekend

In 1997, Will starred in his third consecutive hit summertime movie. Like *Independence Day*, the comedy *Men in Black* featured space aliens, but unlike *Independence Day* it was outrageous and funny. Like his previous hit, *Men in Black* premiered just in time for the Fourth of July. Americans traditionally flock to movie theaters during that holiday, so Hollywood usually releases its biggest films then. After *Men in Black* proved to be yet another box office hit, Smith jokingly began referring to the Fourth of July weekend as "Big Willie weekend."

Men in Black was important to Will for another reason. It helped him return to hip-hop. Only a year earlier he had indicated his retirement from music, but *Men in Black* provided the chance to create a movie's title song. It was an opportunity too tempting to pass up. The song "Men in Black" reached the top of the charts in America, the United Kingdom, and Australia.

Following the success of his hit single, Will released his first solo album, *Big Willie Style*. The album featured several chart-toppers, including "Gettin' Jiggy Wit It" and "Miami." It also contained "Just the Two of Us," Will's tribute to fatherhood. He had returned to hip-hop with renewed energy and style. In both 1998 and 1999, he received the Grammy for Best Rap Solo Performance.

New Beginnings

Despite his hectic work schedule, Will remained in contact with actress Jada Pinkett. They had much in common. Pinkett was born in

Will Smith, accompanied by several young dancers, performs his Grammy-nominated hit "Men in Black" at a rehearsal for the 1998 Grammy Awards show. The theme to his blockbuster movie was his first success as a solo rap artist.

Baltimore in 1971, and like Will she had always known she wanted to be an entertainer. As a teen, she attended the renowned Baltimore School of the Arts. While there, she had become friendly with a young man named Tupac Shakur, who would later become an influential rapper.

In 1991, Jada landed a role on the television show *A Different World*, which like *The Fresh Prince of Bel-Air* was broadcast on NBC. Two years

The hit single "Gettin' Jiggy Wit It" spent three weeks at number one on the Billboard charts in 1998, and enabled Will Smith to win his fourth Grammy Award in 1999. Here, he shows off the award for Best Rap Solo Performance after the awards show.

later, she began taking small parts in low-budget movies, just as Will had done at the start of his film career. Also like Will, she eventually graduated to major motion pictures. Jada's first big role was in the 1996 comedy *The Nutty Professor*, in which she starred opposite Eddie Murphy. She would later have roles in *Scream 2*, the *Matrix* series, and many other films.

The friendship between Will and Jada eventually blossomed into a romance. Each had grown up on the east coast and then worked hard to achieve success in Hollywood. Their similar backgrounds, combined with their upbeat personalities, made them a perfect match. "She's just someone whom I can talk to about anything," Will said of Jada in a 1996 interview with *Ebony*. The couple became engaged in 1997 and married on New Year's Eve of that year.

As the new **millennium** approached, it hardly seemed possible for Will's life to get any better. He was enjoying the rewards of a hit hip-hop album and a string of hit movies. But even better, he and his new bride were expecting their first child together.

Confetti swirls around Will Smith as he begins an outdoor concert in New York City's Times Square to promote his 1999 album *Willennium*. Although not as successful as *Big Willie Style*, Smith's second solo album sold nearly 2 million copies.

5

From Prince to King

Will's first solo album, *Big Willie Style*, had rapidly climbed the charts in both the United States and the United Kingdom. It sold more than 9 million copies in the United States alone. His previous two films, *Independence Day* and *Men in Black*, were ranked among Hollywood's highest-grossing movies ever. Without a doubt, Will Smith was an international superstar.

Life at home was going extremely well also. Jada gave birth to the couple's first child in 1998. It was a boy, whom they named Jaden. Two years later, daughter Willow was born. Will's first son, Trey, was growing up rapidly as well. As he had always promised, Will continued to be an important part of Trey's life.

Will Smith and wife Jada Pinkett Smith arrive at the Nickelodeon Kids Choice Awards in 2005, accompanied by their children. In addition to son Trey (left), Smith is the father of a son, Jaden Christopher Syre, and a daughter, Willow Camille Reign.

Unusual Choices

By 1998, Smith could pick and choose which films he wanted to make. It was clear that moviegoers liked seeing him on the big screen. His last two movies had been science fiction, and although a self-proclaimed science fiction fan, Will was ready for something new.

The film he chose was a hi-tech thriller called *Enemy of the State*. In it, Will plays a Washington attorney who accidentally gets caught up in a tangled web of **espionage** and murder. The role demonstrated Will's emerging talents as a dramatic actor, yet the film was only marginally successful with audiences. It did receive critical praise, however, as a thrilling fast-paced action movie.

The next year, Will made a very unusual choice when he starred in the movie *Wild Wild West*. The movie, based on a 1960s television show of the same name, combined science fiction with the classic cowboy western movie. Although the story was set in the late 1800s, its characters used weapons and technology that did not exist at that time—a particular style referred to as **steampunk**. Will played Captain Jim West, a daring government agent. *Wild Wild West* was an undeniable box-office failure. For the first time, one of Will's movies had earned less money than it cost to make. But with the failure came relief. People would no longer expect magic, and Will could step out from under the pressure of perfection.

Also in 1999, Will released his second solo album. Its title, *Willennium*, took advantage of the worldwide excitement over the coming of the new millennium. *Willennium* did not achieve the overwhelming popularity of *Big Willie Style*, but it sold enough copies to earn a platinum rating. Will's longstanding reputation as a top-rate hip-hop artist was secure.

Smith's next movie, *The Legend of Bagger Vance*, appeared in theaters in the fall of 2000. In this drama, Will was paired with Matt Damon. Despite strong performances by the actors, *The Legend of Bagger Vance* fared poorly. Critics generally felt that the movie was a mere fable, with weak, uninteresting characters designed only to impart a distinct lesson to viewers by the time the credits rolled.

Getting Back on Track

Despite his setbacks, Will refused to abandon dramatic filmmaking. He wanted to prove his ability as a serious actor. That opportunity came in 2001 when Will was asked to play legendary boxer Muhammad Ali.

As an internationally recognized superstar, Will Smith has had the opportunity to mingle with some of the world's most powerful people. Here, he and wife Jada speak with President Bill Clinton, First Lady Hillary Clinton, and their daughter Chelsea as they arrive for the White House New Millennium gala celebration, December 31, 1999.

Interestingly, Will had been offered the role previously but had declined it. He explained why in a 2001 interview with the Knight Ridder news service. "I actually turned down the film for years out of respect for the champ and pure, stark terror of being the guy who messed up the Muhammad Ali story."

When he finally did accept the role, Will dedicated himself to portraying the boxer accurately. He studied video from the 1960s and 1970s to pick up Ali's movement and mannerisms. Smith trained hard in the gym to get into peak physical shape and develop his boxing skills. "There were some rough days," Will said as he described the boxing training. "I got hit every day but you remember the bad ones." The fight scenes in the film were real. Although choreographed

The great boxing champion Muhammad Ali jokes with Will Smith at a premiere for the film *Ali*. Initially, Smith was reluctant to play the iconic figure, but he eventually threw himself wholeheartedly into the demanding part.

beforehand, the actors were hitting one another just like they would have in a real boxing match.

The film *Ali* did not do as well financially as Smith and the production team had hoped. Part of the problem was bad luck. *Ali* premiered just three months after the terrorist attacks of September 11, 2001. It was a time when Americans were distracted by world events. The movie received some unfavorable reviews for being too long. Some critics also mentioned that it seemed more like a funeral than a celebration. However, even the film's critics praised Will for his accurate portrayal of the great boxer.

Ali was a success for Will in several respects. First, it enabled him to finally show the world his dramatic ability. "This is the role I was tailor-made to play," he told Knight Ridder. *Ali* earned Will an Academy Award nomination for Best Actor in a Leading Role. It also gave him the chance to work onscreen with his wife, Jada, who played a love interest in the film.

Familiar Ground

Having accomplished his goal to appear in a serious film, Smith returned to the roles that had made him famous. His next two movies were sequels: *Men in Black II* and *Bad Boys II*. "Some people, once they get an Oscar nomination, they get the bug to only do serious films," he explained to the *New York Daily News*. "For me, I know I'll have time for that, so I didn't want to lose my connection to the youngster in me."

After a three-year **hiatus**, Will also returned to hip-hop. *Born to Reign*, his third solo album, arrived in stores in 2002. That same year, Will also released an album of his greatest hits. The **compilation** included favorites from his solo career, as well as the best songs by DJ Jazzy Jeff & The Fresh Prince.

Will's next summertime blockbuster film premiered in July 2004. It was the fast-paced, futuristic thriller *I, Robot*. The film's title and plot came from a collection of short stories by the late Isaac Asimov, a famous science fiction author. *I, Robot* was set in the year 2035, and Will played Detective Del Spooner. One day while investigating a murder, Detective Spooner discovers a serious problem with the army of robots serving society. Spooner must then fight for his life while attempting to save his city from the robots. Smith jokingly told *Wired*, "It's a city that is doomed. It's not the whole world. I can save a city in my sleep."

Although clearly an action movie, *I, Robot* was more sophisticated than Will's previous summertime hits. It examined how people react differently to progress and technology. "I knew this couldn't be just another summer movie with explosions and chases and special effects," Will told the *Detroit Free Press* shortly after *I, Robot* premiered. "Because audiences have said good-bye to all that. It's been done to death; it's over."

Will Smith greets German fans at the premiere of his 2004 film *I, Robot*. The movie was an international blockbuster, earning over $145 million in the United States and another $200 million in worldwide release.

A desire to make lighthearted movies with a message led Will to his next project, the animated *Shark Tale*. In this underwater adventure, Will provided the voice of Oscar, a lovable fish who learns the importance of telling the truth. *Shark Tale* connected with moviegoers all around the world. As usual, Will was involved with the film's soundtrack.

In 2004, Smith provided his voice for the animated film *Shark Tale*. Many other stars were also involved with the movie, including Angelina Jolie, Martin Scorsese, Renee Zellweger, Jack Black, Peter Falk, and Robert De Niro.

After *Shark Tale*, Smith decided to make a film that would appeal to adult audiences. The romantic comedy *Hitch* debuted just prior to Valentine's Day 2005. Will starred as a "date doctor," who helped **hapless** men court the women of their dreams. It was Smith's third hit movie in less than a year.

In a span of 20 years, Will had gone from small-time rapper to major film star. Along the way, he earned Grammy awards, an Oscar nomination, and a legion of loyal fans. Yet that is not the end of the Will Smith story. In fact, he would probably say that it is only just beginning.

"I Am Hip-Hop" reads Will Smith's T-shirt in this photo taken at a 2005 concert in Florida. Although today he remains very busy with his film projects, he has said that making music remains his first love.

6

Will Smith Today

"There's no experience I've ever had that beats standing in the middle of a stage with 70,000 people and those first couple of seconds of 'Summertime' come on. That feeling is—well, there's nothing like that." Will told *Jet* magazine in 2004, explaining why hip-hop would always be his first love.

Will's busy film schedule could easily prevent him from creating new music, but he refuses to let that happen. He explained to *Jet* that, "as an actor, you're a tool for the director. As a musician, you're exploring and displaying the essence of you." Accordingly, Will has been known to work on his hip-hop albums at night in his hotel room, and sometimes even between takes on the movie set.

In 2005, he released *Lost & Found*, his fourth original solo effort. The album's cover showed a solemn Will leaning against a street sign that reads "West Philly & Hollywood." Presumably, Will was telling his fans that he would never forget his roots, despite his current lifestyle as a movie star. He stated the message even more plainly in the lyrics to "Here He Comes," the album's opening song:

> **For years I been tryin to rip rhymes & get mine**
> **Spit lines, hot like lava this time**
> **I don't got a sitcom to bother with**
> **Or a time conflict with my sci-fi hits**
> **I'm contemplating each statement's wit**
> **& I'm concentrating on making hits**
> **& I'm fittin' em line by line**

Lost & Found featured guest performances by Mary J. Blige, Snoop Dogg, and Will's former partner, Jeff Townes. The album sold reasonably well, achieving gold status, but it fell short of *Big Willie Style* and other past successes.

Answering Critics

A noticeable difference between *Lost & Found* and previous albums was its darker tone. From his earliest days as the Fresh Prince, Will's music had always been bright and playful. But some of the songs on *Lost & Found* were more edgy and serious. For the first time, Will was answering his critics in the hip-hop community.

Criticism of Will's music began in the late 1980s, shortly after he and Jeff Townes attained popularity. Several rappers publicly expressed their opinion that DJ Jazzy Jeff & The Fresh Prince were not true hip-hop artists. They claimed that because the duo's music was humorous and uncontroversial, it did not deserve to be called hip-hop. The criticism was never very loud or widespread, but it seemed to follow Smith throughout his career.

Will always tended to ignore the criticism, instead letting his awards and record sales respond for him. But in *Lost & Found*, he spoke directly to his detractors. In the song "Niceguy," Will mentioned Eminem and other critics by name. He told them, "I'm not your punching bag" and warned, "You better chill before you climb a tree you can't get down." Will went on to explain that writing such lyrics was not his style, but he said, "some stuff a man can't allow."

A harder hip-hop style was not the only change in Will's professional life. He also took a major new step in his filmmaking career. In addition to starring in *I, Robot* and *Hitch*, he had accepted the role of producer for each of those films. This meant that Will had duties to perform behind the camera as well as in front of it, just as he had as a

***Hitch* director Andy Tennant (left) gives instructions on how to play a scene to Smith and his costar, Kevin James. In addition to a starring role in *Hitch*, Smith's company also produced the 2005 film.**

producer of *The Fresh Prince of Bel-Air*. A movie producer must raise money to make the film, hire cast and crew members, and take on many other responsibilities. As far as Will is concerned, accepting new challenges is essential to remaining on top in Hollywood. "The bottom line in this business is, the person who pays the most attention and studies the hardest wins," he told the *New York Daily News* in 2004. "And I refuse to let someone work harder than me."

Will Power

In recent years, Will has become involved in a **multitude** of different projects. In addition to his own films, he also produces the work of other actors and performers. Will owns a production company that develops movies, television shows, and music. He named the company Overbrook Entertainment after his childhood neighborhood. One of Overbrook Entertainment's best-known products is the situation comedy *All of Us*, which airs on UPN. The show was inspired by the lives of Will and Jada and their experiences in raising a family. In 2006, Overbrook produced *Bury Your Dead . . . How I Spent My Summer Vacation*, a reality show chronicling the nationwide tour of rock band Bury Your Dead.

Will's fame and fortune have enabled him to do other types of work as well. He routinely devotes time, money, and energy to improving the lives of others. With Jada, he established the Will and Jada Smith Family Foundation, which works to assist underprivileged families. Its goals are to improve educational opportunities and to prevent violence and drug abuse. The foundation does much of its work in the couple's hometowns, Philadelphia and Baltimore.

Will also does significant charity work in Africa. He became aware of the plight of many African nations while shooting the film *Ali*. Since then, he has labored to help reduce poverty and the spread of AIDS in that continent. In 2004, former South African president Nelson Mandela appointed Will a global ambassador for a major AIDS awareness campaign "He made me understand the power I have as an actor," Will said of Mandela. "He said the platform I have in film is extremely powerful and that I should use it to influence people."

Changing the World—Big Willie Style

Whether he realizes it or not, Will has been influencing people for most of his life. As the Fresh Prince, he and DJ Jazzy Jeff gave many

1997 The film *Men in Black* becomes Will's third consecutive summertime blockbuster. Will's debut solo album, *Big Willie Style*, is released. It contains chart-topping hits such as "Gettin' Jiggy Wit It" and "Men in Black." Will marries actress Jada Pinkett on New Year's Eve.

1998 On February 25, Will is awarded the Best Rap Solo Performance Grammy for his song "Men in Black." He and Jada subsequently have their first child together, a boy named Jaden. In November, Will stars in the film *Enemy of the State*.

1999 Will garners another Grammy in February for "Gettin' Jiggy Wit It." His film *Wild Wild West* premieres in June. His second solo album, *Willennium*, is released in November.

2000 In October, Jada gives birth to daughter Willow, the couple's second child. The following month, Will stars with Matt Damon in *The Legend of Bagger Vance*.

2001 The film *Ali* is released in December.

2002 Will receives an Academy Award nomination for his performance in *Ali*. He releases his third solo album, *Born to Reign*, as well as an album of his greatest hits. The film *Men in Black II* is released in July.

2003 Will reprises the role of Detective Mike Lowrey in *Bad Boys II*, which premieres in July.

2004 Will produces and stars in the science fiction thriller *I, Robot*. He also provides the voice of Oscar in the animated film *Shark Tale*.

2005 The film *Hitch* premieres on February 11. Will's album *Lost & Found* is released the following month. On July 2, he hosts the Live 8 concert in Philadelphia.

2006 Will completes filming *Pursuit of Happyness*, which also features his son Jaden.

Discography

Hit Singles (with DJ Jazzy Jeff)

1986 "Girls Ain't Nothing But Trouble"

1988 "Parents Just Don't Understand"
"Nightmare on My Street"

1991 "Summertime"
"Ring My Bell"

1993 "Boom! Shake the Room"

Hit Singles (solo)

1997 "Men in Black"

1998 "Gettin' Jiggy Wit It"
"Just the Two of Us"
"Miami"

1999 "Wild Wild West" (featuring Dru Hill)
"Will 2K"

2002 "Black Suits Comin' (Nod Ya Head)" (featuring Tra-Knox)

2005 "Switch"

Albums (with DJ Jazzy Jeff)

1987 *Rock the House*

1988 *He's the DJ, I'm the Rapper*

1989 *And in This Corner . . .*

1991 *Homebase*

1993 *Code Red*

1998 *Greatest Hits*

Albums (solo)

1997 *Big Willie Style*

1999 *Willennium*

2002 *Born to Reign*
Greatest Hits

2005 *Lost & Found*

Television

1990–
1996 *The Fresh Prince of Bel-Air*

Films

1992	*Where the Day Takes You*
1993	*Made in America*
	Six Degrees of Separation
1995	*Bad Boys*
1996	*Independence Day*
1997	*Men in Black*
1998	*Enemy of the State*
1999	*Wild Wild West*
2000	*The Legend of Bagger Vance*
2001	*Ali*
2002	*Men in Black II*
2003	*Bad Boys II*
2004	*I, Robot*
	Shark Tale
2005	*Hitch*
2006	*Pursuit of Happyness*

Major Music and Film Awards

1988	Wins Grammy Award for Best Rap Performance
1991	Wins Grammy Award for Best Rap Performance by a Duo
1998	Wins Grammy Award for Best Rap Solo Performance
1999	Wins Grammy Award for Best Rap Solo Performance
2001	Nominated for Academy Award for Best Actor

Cerio, Gregory. "Mister Smith Goes to Stardom." *People* 46, no. 4, p. 64.

"How Will Smith Crossed Over from Hit Rapper to Hot Actor." *Jet* 91, no. 10, p. 56.

Lawson, Terry. "Will Smith Wises Up." *Detroit Free Press*, July 13, 2004.

Lively, Tarron. "Agitated Smith Talks Back." *Washington Times*, April 15, 2005.

Neumaier, Joe. "The Prince Stays Fresh." *New York Daily News*, July 11, 2004.

Nickson, Chris. *Will Smith: A Totally Unauthorized Biography*. New York: St. Martin's Press, 1999.

Norment, Lynn. "Will Smith." *Ebony* 51, no. 10, p. 34.

Ritz, David. "Will Power." *Essence* 23, no. 10, p. 60.

Robb, Brian J. *Will Smith: King of Cool*. London: Plexus Publishing Limited, 2000.

Stuever, Hank. "RoboHero: As Will Smith Again Springs Into Action, He Sees a Gentler Future—for Himself." *Washington Post*, July 11, 2004.

Yarbrough, Marti. "Will Smith Talks about His New Movie 'I, Robot,' His Growth as an Actor & Why Music is His First Love." *Jet* 106, no. 3, p. 56.

Web Sites

www.willsmith.com
Will Smith's official Web site, featuring samples of his latest music, information about his movies, and other biographical data.

www.overbrookent.com
The Web site of Will Smith's production company, Overbrook Entertainment. It contains information about the various projects that Will and his colleagues are currently producing.

www.eonline.com/On/Revealed/Shows/Smith/index.html
A profile of Will Smith by E! Entertainment Television that features many quotes from him.

www.imdb.com/name/nm0000226/
A detailed summary of Will Smith's film career by Internet Movie Database, Inc., including the latest news about his upcoming films.

www.jazzyjefffreshprince.com/index.html
The unofficial Web site of DJ Jazzy Jeff and The Fresh Prince. It contains a wealth of information about the hip-hop duo and their respective solo careers.

accolade—an expression of praise or approval.

aptitude—a natural ability or talent.

compilation—a collection, grouping, or set.

debut—the introductory presentation.

emcee—a master of ceremonies, or host.

espionage—the act of secretly gathering information; spying.

frivolously—done inappropriately and without thought.

genre—a category or style of artistic work.

hallmark—a distinguishing trait.

hapless—unfortunate and pitiful.

hiatus—a gap or interruption in time; a break.

impresario—a showman; a person who produces or promotes commercial entertainment.

medium—a means of communicating or creating.

millennium—a period of a thousand years.

multitude—a very great number.

persona—a character or role that a person displays in public.

philanthropist—a person who devotes time and money to helping others.

spontaneously—without advance preparation.

steampunk—a story that supposes technological advancements using steam-powered and gear-driven technology that did not actually occur. These stories are usually set in the Victorian era or a fictitious Victorian-like modern era.

Jim Corrigan is an established author and journalist who has written about a variety of topics. His books for young readers cover such wide-ranging subjects as American history, cultural diversity, and lifestyles in foreign nations. They include *Europeans and Native Americans* (2002, Mason Crest), *Kazakhstan* (2005, Mason Crest) and *Causes of World War II* (2005, OTTN Publishing). In 2006, Corrigan wrote his first book for adult readers, entitled *The 48th Pennsylvania in the Battle of the Crater: A Regiment of Coal Miners Who Tunneled Under the Enemy*. He resides near Harrisburg, Pennsylvania.

Picture Credits

page

2: Semmer/Face to Face/iPhoto
8: Timothy A. Clary/AFP/ Getty Images
11: Zuma Press/Laura Farr/AdMedia
12: Brian Prahl/Splash News
14: Delalande Raymond/JDD/ GAMMA
17: PRNewsFoto/NMI
19: Splash News/Martin Grimes
20: Everett Collection
22: Potofest
25: Fotos International/Getty Images
28: Michelson/Zuma Press
29: Everrett Collection
30: Michelson/Zuma Press

33: Columbia Pictures/Zuma Press
35: Reuters/Fred Prouser
36: UPI/Michael Larsen
38: UPI/Ezio Peterson
40: Tsuni/Gamma/NMI
42: UPI/Ron Sachs
43: AFP Photo/Lucy Nicholson
45: Franziska Krug/Action Press
46: Eric Liebowitz/DreamWorks/ Zuma Press
48: UPI Photo/Michael Bush
51: Barry Wetcher/Columbia Pictures
53: Reuters/Mike Hutchings
54: Zuma Press/KPA/NMI

Front cover: Lee Roth/Star Max
Back cover: Carlos/INFGoff